# First Science Experiments

## The Amazing Human Body

by **Shar Levine and Leslie Johnstone**

illustrations by **Steve Harpster**

Sterling Publishing Co., Inc.
New York

*For Mia, Paul, and Mark Frank—SL*

*For Joe, Ian, and Jessica Davidson—LJ*

**Library of Congress Cataloging-in-Publication Data**

Levine, Shar, 1953-
  First science experiments : the amazing human body / Shar Levine and
Leslie Johnstone ; illustrations by Steve Harpster.
      p. cm.
  Includes index.
  ISBN-13: 978-1-4027-2437-4
  ISBN-10: 1-4027-2437-3
  1.  Body, Human--Juvenile literature. 2.  Human physiology--
Experiments--Juvenile literature.  I. Johnstone, Leslie. II. Title.
  QP37.L42 2006
  612--dc22

                           2005037679

10  9  8  7  6  5  4  3  2  1

Published by Sterling Publishing Co., Inc.
387 Park Avenue South, New York, NY 10016
© 2006 by Shar Levine and Leslie Johnstone
Distributed in Canada by Sterling Publishing
<sup>c</sup>⁄<sub>o</sub> Canadian Manda Group, 165 Dufferin Street
Toronto, Ontario, Canada M6K 3H6
Distributed in the United Kingdom by GMC Distribution Services
Castle Place, 166 High Street, Lewes, East Sussex, England BN7 1XU
Distributed in Australia by Capricorn Link (Australia) Pty. Ltd.
P.O. Box 704, Windsor, NSW 2756, Australia

*Printed in China*
*All rights reserved*

Sterling ISBN-13: 978-1-4027-2437-4
        ISBN-10: 1-4027-2437-3

For information about custom editions, special sales, premium and
corporate purchases, please contact Sterling Special Sales
Department at 800-805-5489 or specialsales@sterlingpub.com.

# Contents

# Note to Parents and Teachers

Kids probably have more questions about their bodies than about just anything. Can your brain be seen when the doctor shines a light in your ears? Why does your leg twitch when a doctor taps your knee? Children are curious about the world around them and this book is a simple place to start discovering the science of everyday life.

Obviously we can't answer every question your child might ask. This book is a book for young children so all the activities are at a level that can be easily understood and performed by kids. Also, we will not be discussing reproduction or genetics, subjects better covered in books specific to those topics, meant for older ages.

If your child wants to learn more about a specific topic, you can visit the library and find a book on the subject. Surf the Internet with your child and research the question using a search engine where you can type in your question or the topic and be directed to sites which might provide an answer. Make a list or diary of your child's questions and work with your child to find the answers. Think of the things you will discover together.

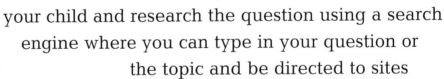

# Safety first

We have tried to make the activities as safe and simple as possible. Some adult supervision is needed with small children, especially when experiments involve anything sharp. Please read these rules with your child before starting any of the activities.

**Do**

✔ Ask an adult before you start if it is ok to do an activity. Some experiments require an adult's supervision and help.

✔ Have an adult handle all glass or sharp objects.

✔ Wash your hands after each experiment.

✔ Keep your work area clean and clean up spills immediately.

✔ Have an adult read the activity with you before starting.

✔ Tell an adult immediately if you or anyone is hurt in any way.

✔ Keep supplies and materials away from younger children and pets.

**Don't**

✔ Do not taste, eat, or drink anything in an activity unless the experiment allows it and an adult gives you permission.

✔ Do not poke yourself with any sharp object or put anything in your nose, mouth, ears, or other part of your body.

# Introduction

There are many ways of looking at your body. The easiest way is to stand in front of a mirror, but you do that every day. In this book we are going to start at the top of your head and work our way down to the soles of your feet. By the time you get to the end of this book you will know your body as well as you know the back of your hand.

But right now there are some things it is important for you to know. Your body is like a complex machine. You have to give it the right fuel, in the form of healthy food and drink, to keep it running smoothly. You need regular tune-ups, so you go to your dentist and see your doctor for vaccinations. It's important to keep clean, so you take baths and brush your teeth often. If a car just sits in the garage, parts start to rust. They seize up and the car stops working. Like a car on the road, you need to be out and active. Exercise will keep your bones and muscles strong and your heart pumping its best. But even machines can't operate at full speed 24 hours a day. You need a good night's sleep, every night. Treat your body with respect. Take good care of it as it's hard to find replacement parts.

# Why is my hair straight when my friend's hair is curly?

Is your hair naturally straight, or curly? After you wash it, does it fall into waves, straight down, or does it frizz up? Do you have the same kind of hair as your brother or sister, or is it more like your mom's or dad's?

## You need

 strands of hair ♦ magnifying glass

## Do this

1. Take a strand of hair from your hairbrush and look at it with the magnifying glass.

2. Now pick it up and hold onto one end tightly with your thumb and index finger. Pull the strand through the same fingertips of your other hand, pressing near your fingernails. Look at the hair with your magnifying glass again. How does the strand look now?

3. Try a hair from your parents, grandparents, or siblings. Ask friends with different types of hair for a strand. What happens?

**4** Use the magnifying glass to compare hair strands: a curly or kinky hair to a straight hair; a hair from a blonde to one from a redhead. Do hairs look pretty much the same? Compare the shaft of each hair, where it comes out of the scalp; what do you see?

## What happened?

Even if your hair is straight, your "pulled" hair is curly. Pulling the strand through your fingertips removed some of the outer layer of the hair, called the cuticle. This caused the hair to curl or kink. The color is caused by pigments called melanins found in the cortex, the middle of the hair shaft—white hair has no melanins so is colorless.

Your hair grows out of the skin on your head through openings called follicles. A follicle is like a cookie cutter—it shapes the hair that grows out of it. If hair follicles are large, the strands of your hair are probably thick. If you have small hair follicles, your hair is most likely fine or thin. Hair type is inherited, so you probably have hair similar to that of your parents or other members of your family.

# How good is my memory?

Some people have "photographic" memories. They remember everything they read or see. You may remember some things but forget others. How good is your memory, and can you do anything to improve it?

## You need

- tray
- dish towel
- several friends
- pens and paper
- clock or watch
- 20 different small objects:
  eraser, pencil, button, coin,
  cork, toy car, stamp, building block,
  spool of thread, ruler, spoon, business card, dice, barrette,
  earring, shoelace, key, nail file, lip balm, magnifying glass,
  whatever else fits on the tray

## Do this

1. Place twenty different small objects onto a tray. Cover them with a dish towel.

**2** Give your friends pens and paper, and tell them they will have two minutes to look at the objects on the tray—but not to write anything down yet.

**3** Uncover the tray and start timing. After two minutes, cover the tray and tell your friends to either print the name or draw a picture of each of the objects.

**4** When they have drawn or printed as many names as they can remember, uncover the tray again to see how they did.

## What happened?

Some of your friends could remember more objects than others. Here are some tricks for improving memory. Try forming groups of related objects: ruler, pencil, and eraser, for example; or barrette, earring, and shoelace—all items you can wear. Another way is to use the first letter of each object to make a sentence: "Eat peanut butter," for eraser, pencil, button. Or imagine the objects in funny positions, such as a business card wearing earrings driving a toy car.

# Why do things look all fuzzy when they get close to my eyes ?

Watch an adult in a restaurant read a menu. Sometimes adults will hold the menu as far away as they can reach. Other times, the menu is right at the end of their nose. If you held the menu that close, the letters would be fuzzy. What's happening?

## You need

♦ table   ♦ masking tape

♦ washable felt tip marker   ♦ helper

## Do this

**1** Ask a grownup to put some masking tape on the tabletop. It should go along the edge from one corner towards the middle.

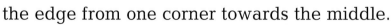

**2** Put your face against the corner of the table where the tape is and look along the tape.

**3** Have your helper move the marker along the tape towards you until the marker point looks fuzzy. Make a mark on the tape at that point.

## What happened?

When the marker point got close to your eyes it looked fuzzy. The point where this happened is called your near point. It is the point where the marker point is so close that your eyes can't see it clearly anymore.

Your near point changes as you get older. Usually children can see things clearly closer than grownups can. Try this activity again with your parent, grandparent, or another adult friend and see if there is a difference!

## Try this

Who can see the farthest? Sometimes grownups are better at seeing things farther away and not as good at seeing things close up.

# Can my nose get tired of smelling things ?

The next time you walk into a bakery, take a deep breath. Doesn't that freshly baked bread smell great? If you stayed there awhile, you'd wonder what happened to that sweet, yeasty odor. Did you use up all the smell, or did your nose get tired?

## You need

- three types of tea (such as Earl Grey, green tea, herbal tea)
- measuring spoon
- three cups or small bowls
- scissors
- paper and pencil

## Do this

1. Place a tablespoon (15 mL) of each loose tea into a clean cup or bowl. If a tea is in a bag, simply cut it open and measure out the tea inside.

2. Sniff each tea and write down any words that would describe what you smelled from each cup.

**3** Now smell the first tea for about two minutes, then take a quick sniff of the second tea. What different odors can you smell in the second tea? Write them down.

**4** Try this again; smell the first tea for about two minutes, and then take a sniff of the third tea. Write down any differences.

## What happened?

When you first sniffed the teas, you noticed some different odors. When you kept breathing in the odor of a single tea for a couple of minutes, your nose got used to the tea smell. Then, when you sniffed a different tea, the odors that were not in the first tea were more noticeable. When you smell the same odors all the time, you learn to ignore them—what you do notice are new and different smells.

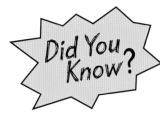

*Did You Know?*

*Dogs have a better sense of smell than people do. Police dogs can find someone who is lost by smelling an article of the person's clothing. They can track criminals from crime scenes, following the scent they give off. The dogs pick out their combination of smells from all the other odors that surround them.*

# Do people with big ears hear better than those with small ears ?

Ears are useful for holding up sunglasses or decorating with earrings. But what's the real purpose for your outer ears? Sometimes called the pinna, the outside part of your ear acts as a collector, bringing sounds into your ears. Could you hear better if you had bigger ears?

## You need

- ◆ 2 letter-size pieces of light card stock
- ◆ 8-inch (20 cm) pie plate or circular cake pan
- ◆ pencil ◆ safety scissors
- ◆ ruler ◆ masking tape

## Do this

1 Place the pie plate or cake pan in the center of each piece of light card and trace around the plate with a pencil.

2 Cut out the circles of card using the scissors.

**3** Use a ruler to draw two crossing lines across the widest part of the circle. Cut along one line to the center.

**4** Overlap the cut edges of the circles to make two cones and tape the card in place.

**5** Cut off the tip of the cones so the ends fit your ears. Hold the cones to your ears and listen carefully. How are the sounds you hear different?

**Note:** Save your cones for another activity—stethoscope.

## What happened?

When you placed the cones to your ears, you probably noticed that the sounds around you were louder. Quiet sounds that you could not hear before, you could hear with the cones. The cones captured more of the sound and directed it into your ears.

*Did You Know?*

*In the days before electronic devices called hearing aids, people used to use a version of what you made to hear better. It was called an ear trumpet.*

# Why do I sometimes almost fall over ?

Babies often fall when they are learning to walk. Kids and adults don't fall down as much, but sometimes it's easy to lose your balance and almost fall. Why is that?

## You need

- ◆ flat floor
- ◆ adult helper
- ◆ old soft pillow
- ◆ scarf or necktie

## Do this

1 Stand straight on a level floor with your feet together and arms down. Do you feel as if you're going to fall? Lift a foot and try balancing on one leg. Now change legs. How did you do?

2 Have your helper tie something over your eyes. Balance on only one foot, then the other. Is there a difference?

3 Place a pillow on the floor in an area clear of furniture or other objects. Have an adult help you onto the pillow.

4 First, just try standing on the pillow. Then lift one foot and try to balance on one leg. Now change legs and try balancing.

**5** Have an adult blindfold you again. Try to balance on the pillow now. Try balancing on one leg, then the other. How do you feel?

## What happened?

You had no problem standing on the flat floor. It was harder to stand on only one leg, especially blindfolded. Moving your hands outward helped. On the pillow, it was harder to keep your balance, especially on one leg or blindfolded. In order to stand and balance you need input from your feet, your eyes, and your brain. You feel the small movements with your feet, your eyes let you see where you are, and your brain makes sense of all the messages sent from your feet, your eyes, and your ears.

## Try this

Put some water in a clear drinking glass. Tip it slightly. The water moves, but the top stays level. Inside your ears are liquid-filled tubes called canals. When your head moves, the fluid moves and disturbs tiny hairs inside your ear. That message goes to your brain, too, to help keep you balanced.

# why do things taste funny when I have a head cold

When you have a stuffy head and a runny nose you probably don't feel like your normal self. And, strangely enough, foods don't taste right either. Is it because of your cold, or is something else going on here?

## You need

♦ apple slices

## Do this

1. Pinch your nose gently with the fingers of one hand so you can't smell anything.

2. Use your other hand to feed yourself a slice of apple. Notice how it tastes.

3. Unplug your nose, and take a sniff of another slice of apple. Notice how it smells.

4. Take a bite of the other apple slice. Does it taste any different than the first slice?

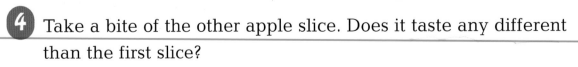

## What happened?

When you couldn't smell the apple it also didn't have a very strong taste. After you unplugged your nose and tasted the apple you probably found that the

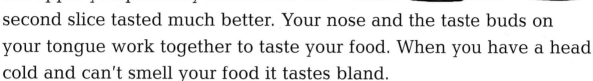

second slice tasted much better. Your nose and the taste buds on your tongue work together to taste your food. When you have a head cold and can't smell your food it tastes bland.

People who have *anosmia* can't detect odors. Those with *hyposmia* don't smell things as well as other people do, while people with *hyperosmia* can smell things better than most people. There are people who can smell everything except for one class of things such as flowers, skunks, or even sweat. While you wouldn't think these conditions may be much of a problem, they are. The nose acts as an early warning system to tell you if a food is rotten, or if something is burning in the kitchen.

# why do I have spit ?

A hungry or really happy dog may try to lick you, slobbering wet gobs of a liquid called saliva all over your face and hands. You don't act that way, but you do have saliva— the stuff you call spit. And the sight and smell of a tasty meal may make us drool, too. But can we find out what saliva does?

## You need

- plain saltine cracker
- slice of bread
- glass of water
- non-starchy food, such as cheese or tofu
- adult helper

**Note:** If a child has a food allergy, use any acceptable non-starch substitute.

## Do this

1 Take a bite of cracker and chew it slowly. Don't swallow. How does the cracker taste?

**2** Keep chewing slowly for a few minutes. How does it taste now?

**3** Take a swig of water and wash down the cracker. Try this again, taking a bite of bread instead of cracker. Experiment with other kinds of food.

## What happened?

The cracker didn't have much flavor at first, but the longer you chewed, the sweeter it became. The cracker contains starch, a chemical made up of lots of smaller pieces called sugars. When saliva mixes with starch, it starts to break the starch down into smaller sugar pieces. Saliva does this because it contains another chemical called amylase, a starch-breaking enzyme. Since sugar tastes sweet, you were able to taste the sugar sweetness in the cracker starch.

**Did You Know?**

*When you are hungry and you smell food, does your mouth fill up with saliva? A scientist named Pavlov experimented with dogs and saliva. He rang a bell before he fed the dogs. After a while, the dogs began to drool when they heard the bell because they thought they would be fed soon.*

# Why are my teeth different shapes?

Look in the mirror at your teeth. Have you lost any of your baby teeth? Why are some teeth long and sharp, while others are short and flat?

## You need

- mirror
- carrot or slice of apple
- slice of bread
- adult helper

**Note:** If a child has any food allergies, substitute the kinds of food.

## Do this

1. Look in the mirror and open wide. Count your teeth. Are there open spaces where you lost teeth?

2. See the chart. How many teeth in your mouth can you match to this picture?

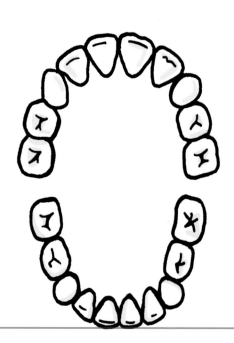

**3** Using your front teeth only, bite off a small piece of carrot or apple and chew it.

**4** Take another bite and chew, but this time use only the teeth on the side of your mouth. Was it easier to bite and to chew?

**5** Now try it using only your back teeth. Which teeth broke up the apple easiest? Which teeth made it easier to chew the apple?

## What happened?

You probably found that your front teeth worked best for biting, but the teeth at the back or side of your mouth worked better for chewing. Children have three kinds of teeth: incisors, canines, and molars. Each type is designed to do a different job. Incisors, at the front of your mouth, are wedge-shaped in order to cut into or slice food. The pointy-tipped canines are used to tear into food. Molars, at the back of your mouth, are for chewing and crushing food.

**Did You Know?**

Before adult teeth come in, most children have 8 incisors, 4 canines, and 8 molars for a total of 20 teeth. Adults have 8 extra teeth called premolars and an extra set of 4 molars called wisdom teeth, giving them a total of 32 teeth.

# Does my skin ever fall off ?

Without skin you'd be in big trouble! You need skin to help protect your insides. Yet, you are losing bits of skin every day. Dandruff, that white flaky stuff on your shoulders, is dead skin.
What about the skin on the rest of your body?

## You need

- ◆ magnifying glass
- ◆ adult helper
- ◆ baby powder or bath powder
- ◆ makeup brush
- ◆ cellophane tape
- ◆ loofah or bath sponge
- ◆ adult helper

## Do this

1. Use a magnifying glass to take a close look at the skin on your hand, arm, leg, and foot. What differences do you see?

2. Ask an adult to spread a thin layer of powder on the back of your hand with a makeup brush. Place a strip of tape over the powder and press it down.

**3** Peel the tape off and lay it on a piece of paper. Use a magnifying glass to look at the tape. Can you see any flakes of skin?

**4** Next time you take a bath, gently use a loofah sponge on one arm but not the other. Once your skin is dry, feel your arms. Which feels softer?

## What happened?

You may have noticed some differences between the skin on different parts of your body. In some places your skin has fine hairs. Other places, such as the soles of your feet, are hairless. Some parts of your skin are smoother than others. When you peeled off the tape on your hand you pulled off tiny bits of loose dry skin. The powder made the shape of your skin patterns easier to see.

The outer layer of your skin is called your epidermis. It is made up of millions of small sections of skin called cells. If you have access to a microscope, look at these flakes of skin and you may be able to see some cells. New skin grows underneath your epidermis and moves up to replace old skin cells that fall off. The newer skin feels softer, so by removing old skin with the loofah sponge you were left with softer skin.

# Is milk really good for my body ?

Do your parents want you to drink more milk? Why is drinking milk or eating certain foods good for your you? What can happen if your body doesn't get the foods it needs? Let's see.

## You need

- large eggshell
- spoon
- milk
- vinegar
- cola

## Do this

**1** Break and separate an eggshell into three plastic cups. Use a spoon to crush each piece of shell into smaller pieces.

**2** Pour some milk into the first cup. It should cover the eggshell.

**3** Pour the same amount of vinegar into the second cup, and pour some cola in the third cup. Now watch the cups for a few minutes. What happens to the eggshells?

**4** Leave the cups and eggshells overnight. Next day, place a strainer in the sink. One by one, pour the contents of each cup through the strainer, rinse with tap water, and tap the contents out onto a piece of paper towel. Look at the three piles of eggshell. Try breaking a piece of each eggshell into smaller pieces.

## What happened?

When you poured vinegar and cola into the cups with the eggshells, you may have seen bubbles form. But nothing happened with the milk. The next day, the shells in the vinegar are thinner and break easily. The shells in the milk are unchanged, but the shells in the soda are now a dull brownish color.

What does eggshell have to do with your body? Both eggshell and your bones contain a mineral called calcium. You need calcium to grow strong and healthy bones. Milk is a good source of calcium. Soda pop doesn't provide calcium. Instead, it contains chemicals that may interfere with the calcium that you take in and cause bones to weaken and break more easily. For strong bones, it's important to drink milk or a milk substitute every day.

# How much air do I take in when I breathe ?

Take a deep breath and hold it. How much air do you think you took into your body? Enough air to blow out all the candles on your birthday cake? Is there a way to measure it?

## You need

- plastic milk jug (gallon/4 L) with lid
- funnel
- 1 cup (250 mL) measuring cup
- black felt marker
- plastic (aquarium) tubing,
- about 3 feet (1 m)
- deep metal roasting pan
- adult helper
- water

## Do this

1 Put the empty jug on a counter and place a funnel in the opening. Fill the cup with water and pour it into the funnel. Use the marker to draw a line on the the jug to show the water level.

2 Don't empty the jug. Measure and pour another cup of water

into the jug. Again, draw a line to show the two-cup (500 mL) water level. Keep adding more water. Mark the level each time until the jug is full. Place the lid on the jug.

**3** Have an adult add several inches of water to the roasting pan, then turn the heavy water-filled jug upside down in the pan. While your helper holds the jug, remove the lid and push one end of the tubing into the jug opening.

**4** Take a deep breath and blow as much air as you can into your end of the tubing. Keep blowing until you have run out of air. Pull out the tubing and have your helper attach the jug lid and turn the jug right side up. Look at the lines you made on the outside. How much water did you blow out of the jug? Can you do better with practice?

## What happened?

Air takes up space. When you blew air into the water-filled container, it forced water out. The amount of air you blew into the jug was the amount or volume of air you had in your lungs. This is called your lung capacity.

# what kinds of sounds does my heart make ?

Lub dub. Lub dub. That's the sound of your heart beating. You can't put your ear to your chest to hear it. You need something like a stethoscope. That's a piece of medical equipment that lets you listen in on your heartbeat. You don't have one handy? We can help.

## You need

- plastic soda bottle
- scissors
- ear cone (from experiment, pages 16–17)
- 1-foot (30 cm) length of rubber hose
- electrical or duct tape
- adult helper

## Do this

**1** Have an adult cut the pop bottle in half with the scissors. Cover the cut end of the top piece with tape to make it smooth.

**2** Tape the hose to the mouth of the bottle and the tip of the cone inside the other end of the hose. This is your stethoscope.

**3** Place the bottle end just below your left nipple on your chest.

That's where your heart is. Place the cone near your ear. Can you hear your heart beating?

**4** Try it on a friend. Place the cone in your ear and the bottle over their heart. Save the stethoscope for another experiment (see pages 40–41).

## What happened?

You could hear your heart beat. The top of the soda bottle funnels the sound into the hose and the ear cone makes the sound louder so you can hear it. Your heart is a pump. Blood flows into your heart from other parts of your body and your heart pumps it through the four sections of the heart and out again to your lungs and your body. It's the closing of the valves between the parts of your heart that causes the sounds you hear in your stethoscope.

**Did You Know?**

The valves in your heart allow the blood to flow in only one direction. If the heart valves don't work correctly, it causes a different sound called a murmur. If you become ill because a valve is not working properly, doctors can replace the valve with a mechanical one. People can live long and healthy lives with mechanical heart valves.

# How can I tell how fast my heart is beating?

When you finish a race or run for a goal in soccer or football, you probably notice that your heart is racing, too. Exercise makes it beat faster. How much faster? That depends on how hard you were exercising. Try this and you can see how fast your heart is beating.

## You need

♦ modelling clay   ♦ toothpick   ♦ adult helper

## Do this

1 Roll a small bit of clay into a ball about the size of the end of a pencil. Flatten one side of the ball. Push the flat end of a toothpick into the domed side of the clay ball.

2 Do about 20 jumping jacks or run in place for about a minute.

3 Hold out your arm and have an adult balance the ball of clay on your wrist, where you can see veins under the skin. You may need to move it around to find the spot with the most movement.

**4** Watch the tip of the toothpick as it moves back and forth. Count the number of times it moves.

**5** Take off the pulse meter and run in place or try more jumping jacks. Put the pulse meter back on and see if moves faster.

## What happened?

The toothpick moved back and forth along with your pulse. Each time your heart beats it pumps blood out to your fingertips and the little surge of blood gives you a pulse. When you are resting, your heart beats slowly. If you exercise, your heart will beat more rapidly. Kids' hearts beat faster than adults', and heart rate slows with age. Normal resting heart rates in babies can be as high as 160 bpm (beats per minute). Kids from 1 to 10 have normal rates between 70 to 120 bpm. From age 10 to adult, the range is 60 to 100 bpm. Well-trained athletes can have rates from 40 to 60 bpm.

*Did You Know?*

*The oxygen in your blood is carried by red blood cells. You have about twenty-five trillion (25,000,000,000,000) of these cells in your body. Each cell lives for about 120 to 130 days and then it needs to be replaced. The marrow, deep in your bones, makes about 90 million of these cells every minute.*

# Are my fingerprints the same as my toeprints ?

Look at the edges of door frames in your house. Do you see tiny patterns left by some child who had dirty fingers? Check out the tips of your fingers. Who do you think put those marks on the walls?

## You need

- ◆ soft pencil
- ◆ white paper
- ◆ cellophane tape
- ◆ magnifying glass
- ◆ soap and water
- ◆ adult helper

## Do this

1. Use a soft pencil to make a 2-inch (5 cm) square on some paper. Fill it in, making a thick, black surface.

2. Rub a finger over the black square, then press the finger on a clean piece of white paper. Can you see any lines or patterns? (Wash your hands.)

**3** Rub a different finger in the square. Have an adult place some cellophane tape over the dirty fingertip, then peel off the tape. Lay the tape next to the first print. Are their patterns the same?

**4** Try it again, but this time rub your big toe in the square. Take a cellophane tape print of your toe. Place this print next to your fingerprint. (Don't forget to wash that toe!) Do the prints look the same? Use a magnifying glass to compare them.

**5** Take prints from family and friends. How do your fingerprints compare to theirs?

## What happened?

You discovered that you can make finger and toe prints and they don't look like those of your family or friends. Every person has a unique set of finger and toe prints. Prints have ridges that can be arranged in three kinds of patterns. Loops have ridges that look like many "C" letters piled next to each other. Arches look like tiny hills, and whorls look like spirals or circles.

Arch

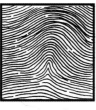
Tented Arch

Left Loop

Right Loop

Whorl

# If a mosquito is so tiny, how can I feel it land on me ?

Are you ticklish? Do you giggle when someone lightly touches you? Some parts of your skin are more sensitive to touch than other parts. Let's see just how sensitive to touch you are!

## You need

- 2 paper clips
- ruler
- masking tape
- pencil and paper
- helper

## Do this

1. Straighten a part of the paper clips.
   Tape them to the ruler 2 inches (5 cm) apart so the wire ends poke out one side. It's a touch tester.

2. Have your helper gently touch your palm with the tester. Don't look to watch what your helper is doing. Have the helper move one wire closer to the other on the ruler and touch your palm again. Keep doing this until you can no longer feel two separate touches from the wire ends.

**3** Measure the distance between the wire ends, using the ruler. Write down the distance for your palm.

**4** Try the tester on the back of your hand, on your leg and arm, on your back, and on your fingertips. Write down the distances between the wire ends for each part. The closer together you feel the wires, the more the sensitive area of skin you are testing. Where is your skin the most sensitive?

## What happened?

Some areas of skin, like your fingertips, are very sensitive and can feel the ends of the two wires very close together. Other areas of skin, like on your back, are less sensitive so the wire ends need to be farther apart to feel two separate touches. The distance between the two wires at which you can still feel two separate points is called the two-point threshold.

**Did You Know?**

Pain is your body's way of alerting you to danger. When a mosquito bites, the pain lets you know about it. What causes the pain? The mosquito's saliva contains a chemical to keep your blood liquid while it sucks the blood up. This chemical irritates your skin, so it hurts.

# Why does my tummy growl or grumble when I am hungry ?

When lunch or dinner is late, does your tummy rumble or make funny noises? What is going on down there? Let's find out.

## You need

- tennis ball, orange, or grapefruit
- old pair of leggings or tights
- stethoscope (from experiment, pages 32–33)

## Do this

**1** Place a round object into the opening of the leggings or tights. Twisting the end of the clothing, begin squeezing and moving the ball down the leg towards the toe end.

**2** Use both hands to squeeze, pushing the ball down the hose. Try it again, this time using a larger round object. Is it harder to move this to the toe end of the leggings?

**3** Now place the soda bottle part of the stethoscope on your tummy near your belly button and listen. Move your stethescope back and forth to listen on all sides of your belly button.

## What happened?

When you are hungry, you make more spit. So you won't drool you swallow it—and you swallow air along with your saliva.

Normally, when you eat, food gets ground up in your mouth then moves down a tube called your esophagus into your stomach. There the food mixes with chemicals that help break it down. When it leaves your stomach, food and air is pushed through your intestines by muscles. This movement through tubes is called peristalsis. Pushing the ball through the tights is much like how your muscles move food through your esophagus and intestines. You may have been heard food and air bubbles moving through your intestines when you listened with the stethoscope. When you're hungry, you can sometimes hear a grumbling sound even without a stethoscope—and others nearby may hear it, too.

# What makes a tummy ache?

It's great to be a kid! The only time you get a tummy ache is usually when you've eaten too many treats. Adults aren't as good as you are when it comes to breaking down food. Let's see why grownups get stomach aches more than you do.

## You need

- 2 drinking glasses
- vegetable oil and olive oil
- teaspoon
- water
- liquid dishwashing detergent
- adult helper

## Do this

1. Half fill each of the glasses with warm water. Place a drop or two of oil into each glass.

2. Have an adult add a teaspoon (5 mL) of dishwashing liquid to one of the glasses.

**3** Use a spoon to stir the glass with the dishwashing liquid until it is mixed and frothy. Use a clean spoon to stir the glass with the oil. What does the liquid in the two glasses look like?

## What happened?

The oil stayed together in the glass with the water. In the glass with the dishwashing liquid the oil was no longer in a single blob. Chemicals in the dishwashing liquid called emulsifiers split the blob of oil into tiny droplets. When you eat oils or fats, they go through your esophagus into your stomach. Then they go into your intestines. In your intestines, chemicals called lipases act like the dishwashing liquid to break down the fats you eat into smaller parts that your body can use. As people grow older, the chemicals in their intestines don't digest oils and fats as well as they used to when they were younger.

Did You Know?

*Rub your stomach. If your hand is below your belly button, you've got the wrong place. That's where your intestines are. Your stomach is above your waist, under your ribs on your lefthand side.*

# Why does my knee jerk when the doctor taps it?

Did your body ever do something that you didn't expect? If you have ever had a doctor test your reflexes with a rubber hammer, you were probably surprised when your arm lifted or your leg moved all by itself. Let's see why.

## You need

◆ chair   ◆ adult helper   ◆ your body

## Do this

**1** Sit in a chair and cross one leg over the other. Don't turn yourself into a pretzel, just cross your legs so that the back of the knee of the top leg is balanced on the knee of the bottom leg.

**2** Ask your adult helper to kneel or crouch beside you. Make sure your helper is not standing in front of your leg.

**3** Have your helper raise a hand and make a chopping motion, gently tapping it against the soft part of your leg, just below your kneecap. Only use the hand, never any other object. It's not necessary to do this with much force; just a light tap will work.

4 Trade places with the adult and see if you can get his or her leg to move.

## What happened?

This is called a knee-jerk reflex, because your knee jerks automatically; you can't stop it from happening. It just pops up when it is tapped. Reflexes happen without your having to think about them. A signal is sent from the nerves in your knee to your spine. Then another signal is sent back to your leg. At the same time, a signal is sent to your brain where you realize what is happening; but by that time it is too late, you have already moved your leg.

Now that you know what a reflex is, what other ones do you think your body has? For example, you cannot keep your eyes open when you sneeze. When you were first born you had something called the Morrow reflex; if someone brushed your cheek you would turn and try to suck on something. Another reflex is the Babinski reflex. With this, if someone gently strokes the center of your foot the toes on your feet curl. Another reflex is your gag reflex that protects your airway and stops food going into your lungs.

# How fast am I growing?

Sometimes you meet a relative or a friend of your parents and they gush and say, "My, how you've grown!" It doesn't seem to you that you've changed much, but how can you tell? Here's a way to keep track.

## You need

- ◆ felt marker
- ◆ large roll of paper
- ◆ adult helper
- ◆ 4 heavy books

## Do this

**1** Have an adult roll out a long piece of paper; the brown kind used for wrapping packages would be perfect. You'll need about 6 feet (2 m). Heavy books can hold down the edges.

**2** Lie down on the paper, so that the bottoms of your feet are even with the bottom of the paper.

**3** Have an adult use a felt marker to trace around your body and outline your shape. Place the date you did this on line.

**4** Roll up the paper and put in a safe place, or ask to have the chart hung up someplace. Repeat this activity on the same paper every 6 months.

## What happened?

You made a growth chart. Instead of just knowing how many inches in height you gain in a short period of time, you also have a way of showing how your shape changes over the years. Kids grow on average about 2 to 2½ inches (5 to 6 cm) each year. When they reach adolescence they have a growth spurt for a year or two when they can grow several inches—and not just upward but outward. Most people stop growing in height in their late teens or early twenties. How tall you will eventually grow to be depends on several things. First, it depends on how tall your parents are, because tall parents usually have taller children than shorter parents. Your diet and health problems can also affect your growth.

# Index